Planned Solstice

KUHL HOUSE POETS

edited by Jorie Graham *and* Mark Levine

Planned

Solstice

Poems by DAVID MICAH GREENBERG

UNIVERSITY OF IOWA PRESS  Iowa City

University of Iowa Press, Iowa City 52242

Printed in the United States of America
http://www.uiowa.edu/uiowapress

The publication of this book was generously supported
by the University of Iowa Foundation.

Printed on acid-free paper

Library of Congress Cataloging-in-Publication Data
Greenberg, David Micah, 1972– .
    Planned Solstice: poems / by David Micah Greenberg.
        p.   cm.—(Kuhl House poets)
    ISBN 0-87745-858-8 (pbk.)
        I. Title.   II. Series
    PS3607.R448P58 2003
    811'.6—dc21   2003042645

03   04   05   06   07   P   5   4   3   2   1

THIS BOOK IS FOR SARIT.

CONTENTS

ACKNOWLEDGMENTS

Some earlier versions have appeared in *Ploughshares*, the *New Republic*, and the *Colorado Review*. Some quotations in "All My Days" are from *On the Altar of Freedom: A Black Soldier's Civil War Letters from the Front* by Corporal James Henry Gooding, edited by Virginia M. Adams. Thanks to Peter Sacks, Wayne Koestenbaum, Mark Strand, Jorie Graham, and Allen Grossman for sustaining kindness.

I

HABITAT

What incident to start with, incident of research
adamantine: serviceberry, shellbark, gathering maples
staghorn red sumac, wordless pattern.

Morning is riven in starting. When patterned
in research, lilacs stand in the calm many-bodied lake.
What face should appear in it?

Equal in light, the hemlock will temper
branch above water. Loose birds bead their song
waiting in the lake. But democracy is not awakening

contrasts. I want a new voice
that is not imitation but description, could strip
the cattails of their thin muzzle, the sun of its brown

sheen today. The ferns by the water, half turned up,
touched, have taken root near a patch of drying
sharp broad grass. I part them and find

a hardening sound, a buzzing, egglike, clump.
Next to it a pod has split as cross sections of a ship.
This is the course of the water as it comes down from waiting:

with a rustling sound like thickening, water falls on pools
water the same level as the sky
chained of morning, half-chained; a day is enough.

In disagreement and sympathy origins
countenance daily the ever-stricken plan
whose conclusions seem inevitable only from that course.

Water and arch, in arched meadows of sea
green divides the swells, green committees
riding the skin of nations, riding down and flaying it down
the St. Lawrence, to Indians the Canada, which is Canada.

THE HOLE IN THE OCEAN

Hovering in the air were two luminous shapes.
They turned, balanced in a pose of surrender. Water
poured into the lower world, in channels
unsolved by busy tides and fish.
Then a phrase of music is misheard, and the green
Orpheus descends and strikes
a counterweight to time rising beatifically.

With the more subtle water of routing
revelation is wet in skein.
There is no closing, the sluice burns
diachronic steel through funnel coral.
So Marines barge in and settle.
The end of the choice proves two stars
are covenant and listen to the growing music apart.

COMMON WILL

I

Pleasure is the widow, circulating.
She walks and her dress unfolds like a stream
folds in clear seams. The willow streams
down the bank. Where she walks the stream flashes
windows, a creed of windows. She weeps through
river, the metal of the answer. Pleasure is the widow.
So some pleasure is misspent. So the burnished
river pulls in a bed of wind.
Because she has not gained in the question

2

In the line of trees part of a mirror grows
through a harder forest. Pallor
is storm, a middle of rain sours its skin.
We hear marble water dressing; we remember
where the garden planned. The rain faces readiness,
glass, grayer in shirred country as color comes
afterlife with need scrawled in it
natural and artificial fire.
Red trees hang night north and south.

Weber: 'if at the beginning of a shower a number of people on the street put up their umbrellas at the same time, this would not ordinarily be a case of action mutually oriented to that of each other, but rather of all reacting in the same way to the like need of protection' a meeting mark although in almost soviet circumstance this is also what patronage endures — the humbling, integer of will. The sensory pragmatism, a loss of risk in peripatetic orchard. What works has a deeper appreciation for what does not.

4

Consciousness
combs with the sterile
shalelike concentric accumulation of remainder.
A light in already clear
waters, as advancement a median of the ever ready
tears in nine light
unanswered change, and brings dissolution.
The cemetery wheel of citizenship,
a theory of chance will not change.

SCHOOLYARD WITH BOAT

"The child plays at being not only a shopkeeper
or teacher but also a windmill and a train."
—Walter Benjamin, "On the Mimetic Faculty"

Our horizon thickened, dropped lower like grain.
There was no grain. And it was dawn again.

Waves darted out of the snow, turned to wind.
The snow waved as out a flawed window.

The wind made odd furrows through the field.
There was no time between lines.

Dawn and not, reflected presently.
Culled, the snow overturned and was now.

What when not, repeated the wind. Children
pulled in a blind row against it.

The resilience of children grows
with the instability of progress.

When bright snow sheared and dulled
I believe no matter. No note guards the gate.

✳   ✳   ✳

Negation in retrospect, although not prospectively
culls in 'scape' the grating of canvas or progress.

Not words alone pleased me, said the flag
lines will not meet. The white cord chimes on the pole.

Not words alone the flag hangs, knowing
held back, as uncertainty means negation

struck down, the corrective open to learning
is sustainable in ignorance.

A gull a prospective self
billeting in the wind is resistance, in a mind

knowing resistance and measuring in it
progress, self-iterative spanning. The gull sweeps

belief. But what <u>learns</u>? Not what is to be learned. What learns —
when snow folds on threshing snow

when the lesson is valuable
gain will not cull in loss, snow is a thorn of it.

The snow on brick chalks and thins.
Red lines and white are drawn together.

Children brace by succeeding each other
in the wind, eyes shut to glare.

The gull sweeps and its shadow into snow
furls — a steel share

as snow is in breathing motion like a bird
shaking snow from crest.

Miseducation risks correction within its own
frame. A crop

is a decision of field. Harbinger of space, white winter,
work with me while I live. When I do not, do not work.

ANNA BOOK OF A

Aesclapius sometimes *became* a snake.
What medicine practices, inverts

as instrument. His fingers combine, throat widens into a mouth.
He is a swallowing
(his wand untwines, loosens, presses into a human face).

Colored in black bands
unguent — undulating

the sudden thickness of the snake
elides in a feeling ray of misprision.
Its stricture met whole as uncertain

laudable green sense, sharing its tidal suspicion.
Where the animal meets it kills as it tried.

A third develops from thicker stem:
he pries up and chokes where neck hide softens to flesh.
A lathered bone

walls (the advent) press the visible.
Roaming with walls waist high, the animal peers down.

He believes he becomes what he sees.
He is in the undivided clinical scales, the carriage of hanging.
Nothing else is inside its walls.

Like the word *Minotaur*, medical language means just what it is
hemolysis (wand a scaling

identification — passion with denunciatory
wholeness, a mask grove moves in lineament
paler than the satisfying

a sickness of citizenship with care).
ACS took x's children when she did not leave her batterer.

By a shelter
water rats and pheasants swam up from the East River.
You have a name.

LANDBRIDGE

Two animals on a radiating tree
race in long peeling hyacinth-like bulbs;

lightning shears as minuteness, evergreen, ever-brown
abbreviation, killing in thickness what the mind sets.

It builds under high wishing cranes.
Eye and hooked fur streak, shaking the branch

in dialogue between jackal-headed baits.
Three bones move from jaw to middle ear. Lightning snaps behind.

It turns thin soil into tunnels. Sparrow hands
will not sail. Splints

enclose a brick smokestack with radio antennae on top
warehouse emptiness of movie lots.

A lobster wholesaler on the channel
gushes floorboards.

Their race is not social pollution, white sheets across the horizon.
It is difference, who speaks, and chance, who listens.

65 million years is each death in the middle passage.
It turns a trench in the harbor

repentant in planning
a habitless credit:

it is yucca.
Stubbed white flowers narrow as they widen, listening surviving its mate.

Thin aloe hears
each possible, human, sunless circle, an egg in the blue,

withering what endures and what survives.
The narrowing is not hope; everything possible is human.

WALTZ GOURD

In the alley a rat tried to assemble a pig.
Weeds licked the rat. In healing
bolts, the rat licked the pig. Fireflies
drew lines over grass, in a revision.
The rat said, I would feel freer on the whole
with a larger pig. Needles rest in a bitter smell
of decomposed leaves, patterned in rain.

News — the medical miracle has a tail
between the eyes. Look then to life;
it has no part in races that consume.
When the rat came with a sickle and mowed the
constellation of the great commoner the pig
cornflowers grew blue stars, and ability
threaded automaticity and clearing skies.

WAR GOURD

I

Unvisaged ability is a winter garden.
Mooring wastes what may simply save it.
The garden attracts terror to terror
cultural metaphrasis
organic abrasiveness.
The well in precision is hastened by design
sand in soil driving
hastening the medicinal horror.
It seals the indefinite forever in blood certainty.
The mood moon appeals
a middle clarity of unconditional knots.
War will never bring rebirth, but snow settles counsel as trust.

2

Nebulaic violence, settlement and red sinew
takes the inverted claims to heart.
Intention relived as consciousness
coincident with melted trust
solders in fingers — opposed or even the gull flare.
Warlike memory, a fire knob
occasions what may be declined
first in ritual as evades promptness.
What is unclear will mean nothing more than solitude.
Attention, constellation less precise
whose instrument is the only in a level sea
navigation continues even as eyes.

CRAZING GOURD

The conscious vine stained cuneiform
resin as a sun-like order
decays and ferments.
Wide rows of mouth, grapes in milk and dust
wild patterns — a continous vine, future
impermeable reactive slugs in fixed array.
I was drunk without knowing it, and seen.
By elms sat the avoided
few.
Fringed pods saw *me*.
A rupture in path is a vine
blindness whose organic alleviation still
grew
friendship with contradictory descriptive reserve.
The hill pooled in a concave grove.
I was dismissed in familiar terms,
persuasion, panned-down in unfamiliar terms.

*   *   *

There was clustered building, soil
boring, caissons to bedrock.
One — a hole in use
cavern two a hole in usefulness.
Girders were guided to girders
which is anxiety and the serious radar chain of
commitment.
A river went across its site.
If unconscious time mattered, an ensign of completion, the *assigned*
promised a shark-finned, earnest, seating plan of the god.
Under the river (that middle generation) grew
plastic charitable gain
in coarse mixture
hops, grist, sea-wing
atmospheric star joists, stretcher, header, soldier, shiner
used, unused in rivering hand — a zero mark, water that is not level.

*   *   *

Comedy, a sugar tree
warm as shame is to identity
grows cold, exculpatory
grandiose. Seriousness — and not guilt — grants privacy.
Men and women go back to work.
The watchers stay in their vine.
There is no middle way. Here is the fist of sun, and of rain.

2

FOUR STONES

I learned I must change. The rain clicked around morning, a breadlike
mantle, becoming unexplained, unimplored
wedded, stamina of light.
Was lightning worth shelter?

Wind pointed all leaves one way.
Wet leaves a darker green, green water pearled. If strain between did not yield
the Atlantic, I still listened to choice.
Thunder went down the mountain, I counted no other freedom

time's interregnum, mountain and sea. There was a series of lives —
the converse readying of time
fury the almost notched strangulation but who knows when it was dead
black tide

is yes social but has a current through it, windless storm.
Tapers of bells down mesh rays, the little year baked spring
changing green for rigor. I read while waiting. French peasants, from S. of the
    Loire,
came to Port Royal in 1606. Many were engagés, bound

to trappers for five years, a pause between what was logical
and natural.
They stopped every week
work before rest, a calculating abundance, passion without hope,

pebbles shrouded in clear water, evolutionary, transpiring;
Acadians diked and drained sea marshes. Coastal routes directed
civil warfare between d'Aulnay and de la Tour's companies.
Hornblend in rock, refusing to convert Micmacs, expelling Jesuits to Isle
    Mont-Desert

both settlements burned by a single ship from Jamestown, anticlerical,
their science without figures
dissolved.
Internal suits rose as conflict with the British,

their contentiousness halted colonial courts, then a misunderstood oath,
the cormorant's eye a glass gem.
Split red, soldiers asked to meet Acadian men
then jailed them, their families separated, fed shoes and spoilage the 1755

winter. Survivors had children sold by judges for loitering,
without connection
crowning sediment, means and ends breathing,
Beausoleil promised to slit every throat of new settlers

—this the story of 12,000, fewer than a single Bosnian town—
a mild abbreviation, their moving ballast, and no more war.
When relocated to rural Pennsylvania
they saw themselves prisoners of war and did not work.

Maryland's governor arrested 'papists who incited slave revolt,'
proving them to live elsewhere; in France
died in smallpox quarantine at St. Malo on the sea.
Change is wrought in links, when chains cover their forge.

There was another way, not good enough for me
—the capacity to criticize self as a substance—
public love; yet I couldn't move backward.
Two boats, then Beausoleil's, stopped in N. Orleans on route to Quebec

praising him who quiets the faceless who look foreward.
Their movement restricted by the Spanish governor until 1769,
unreceived, unequivalent, eventually racist, with their boot
toe pointed, nothing unspeakable in their wake.

Parent, I was held of another grace.
White sails uncovered me; I was kept on shore as their authority
held in pointed, brackish
time. It reminded me when I was enough. It traveled

change, and there might be no abeyance, a separate
past. It meant clarity.
I guarded what I didn't know, constant water, so its need grows.
It marked where the grave was, and knew if Mladic was dying.

On its cover
I sketched a column with a pale maze of trees on top,
branches crossing. The column became a real tree, greening to a striped maple
as the eye went up, but never in my defense. I was here;

what could the burning grass *do*? So I chose
the light, kind fire, killing the accident; the morning,
its gradation of judgment; the antagonistic, athletic, vehicular
mind, spindled like the dawn and morning rotate.

3

ALL MY DAYS

I

What happens matters more than what I chose. We meant *in place* as helplessness — what ground follows us then? A swaying in region, within as without. This is where the grass would lie differently. Here is a three-thorned season. Narrative comes after commitment, and generalization postpones it. But prior and prospective commitments are as bark to skin, given what we still see. Clara Barton — 'We have captured one fort — Gregg — and one Charnel house — Wagner — and we have built one cemetery, Morris Island,' its outer walls some inner garden. We live in a waking sway — concrete in the tree. Henry Gooding — 'it is here without definite prospect of accomplishing its mission.' Having woken (love of war) without categories he is still stricken with experiential quality, actors, opposition, disorganization, and human means. Vision is discord in possible and historical suns since the beginning, and never enacts what it sees. Gooding — 'What better reward is possible to conceive than the blessings of those we left behind in sorrow.' Gulls line up on pier remains; others point into crates. Segment in ranger found. A man shot into the sand.

Without chance of common sacrifice, a covenant of birds — blue-clawed osprey, potters-plume, rails and plover — tightness I tried to lift, and said it was nothing. A barn owl's bacterial mottling, the sun-pretending bird on poison bottle, 'a glyph-like combination of hand and face,' the regiment refused partial raises 'as we have always done, before and since that day we were offered to sell our manhoods for ten dollars per month,' not reliving what I *and others* had won, in success and circularity of will. The wind is turning wetter and more sour. Where I felt more at home, strained by conditions in which they found themselves, curfew and lights dimmed for those who should not have been there (perspective and context as one). Gooding — 'Between the columns there was a space of eight paces for the funeral cortege to pass in review before the troops' a self-freed slave, sister and mother still enslaved. 'A man dies none the less gloriously, standing at his post on picket, or digging in the trench; his country needs him there, and he is as true a soldier.' Past the WTC, she turned to greet, in a high distracted voice, "God bless you God bless you! People worried for what I was doing with her, God bless them." God told her to move — her case worker cried. "Life is good!" She said about her sign and job: "I happy lady. People know I and happy sign — one" and will claim voice in opposing us, nakedly as professionally. But lives which need no sacrifice to be seen — hasten the day. The north wind lights electrically. He slapped a dog.

3

A level gate of fire, one day. 'Why come as spectators when you can become actors?' Without denominational limit, stones in field, reach human work and division. General Strong—'Aim low and put your trust in God.' A funnel narrowed to a single point—an unbelievable, slow, siren—reclined among saints. "Our pastor eloped with a 14-year-old girl, who died giving him twins." Yes or no as *both* is free in time but static as image within its sun plane, corona and decision. Pain, even through God-given discursion the bursae veinous into revolutionary severence, plans if not reconstitution then for bodily competence. These are the crossroads where suicides are buried. A second commandment, hands will not love what they make a condition of creation, the saline one-colored pain. The UN school was a women's shelter on 52nd street, where two hundred women with severe mental illness lived—a Sudanese immigrant, wry, angry, and brilliant, under imagined suspicion for bombing the Kenyan embassy; this hopes for every witness compromised by suffering, as the flat sunway. 'Every rebel magazine blown up is considered a gain to the Union cause, in the same light of the 'utter demoralization' of such existing in this or that section, and many persons are credulous enough to believe that all such natural combinations will end the war, instead of good hard fighting' just war and just peace laid parallel like remains, girding suffering. I had too great needs for more than one person.

The day in shearing is made too far ahead, and he must choose the standard.
A soldier who before enlisting almost killed himself, killed three men,
medusa-lion. Caroline would say, 'All right. Mr. x.' Sigh. 'Mr. x is a 47 year
old . . . one day, he found himself . . . and then . . . ' a life in miniature, and
won what was least resolvable. She died helping displaced men and women
in Lower Manhattan; her integrity saw my suffering toward social suffering,
and I failed in seeing kindness as reproach. One or many is not insolvable,
but a matter of priority, as spray reneges, sails crossed: wrapped sails. In
New Bedford, a lighthouse takes sun from water. A machine house, the stem
of a crane plies. Gooding wrote not to be buried at sea, that 'Friends, they
may gaze where I am laid so low' hissing a dryness as inland, the conclusion
siphon. Unshared waters involve strategies of trust. With so many families in
one site, dig deep the first grave, and unforged variety. After the assault failed
they captured W.'s pickets, of five black men. Two were sharpshooters. One
claimed he owned slaves. 'Blood, mud, water, brains and human hair melted
together; men lying in every possible attitude, with every conceivable
expression, their limbs bent into unnatural shapes by the fall of 20 or more
feet.' Hallowell was castrated and a bullet drove Jewett's own sword into his
head. Where patience will not climb, the inner wall Union guns from sea and
Confederate within shot them.

James Henry Gooding
five years whaling in India and the Arctic Ocean,
joined the 54th Massachusetts regiment in New Bedford.
The regiment moved to Florida, where they
defended Seymour from his incompetence.
Grace wrote the talented Gooding was killed.
He was not. He survived to Andersonville

compelled to weave like the day

4

INTEREST

Is it the remains of *another* house?
The fountain a foundation wall
is transparency a storm of weal.
House
terrace and J-shaped clearing, look to island salvages.
An apple tree, three-trunked, with tufts —
the rough wall which collapses but is mostly firm,
chimes,
a Chinese character lattice. "There is no end, but addition."
A brick chimney ends in a ceramic spout.
Reconstructing taste is organic calculus
eight
trunked. White frames lift up level slopes
on Cape Anne, evidence
massive capital retained in setting forth company.
Here
preservation is not a test past readiness.
There is a mocking bird
its static floodlight call unanswerable by one bird.
Eye
oil-soaked with plenty
numbers as 'many' and as 'one,' water
tract a c-curve the ministering wing.
Continuity
convinces us rest is irreducible silence.
Under a four-foot-long horizontal spider strand
a wasps' nest — undisturbed in the hedge — a mummy-sack
preserved,
a cedar St. Francis runny vertical piety and large hands.
A dove greets. No one can follow its privacy.

A calligraphic retinue of remediation
carves
at ceiling parallel leaves and waves
as source castigated by agreeable sin.
A thicket of two singing birds in orchard scrabble
a war
flag tile, it is for itself. You may be the same.

ZERO COTTAGE

We walked Rock Creek to Georgetown
wilderness cultivated in self-preservation.
We reach a shelter with prints of plants, photographs
serious men in a cordial
row.
Green bronze on green grass
tuned, water in a sloped basin
— the sieve of statesmanship
assessing failure.
Ferns, fronds, a low-hung Orangery, bark stripped from budding
late-June rose sinew
an exponential canvas, green, brown, gray
in description — the specificity of caring and not caring precede
symmetry.
"Peace, like liberty, requires constant devotion and ceaseless vigilance" —
    Cordell Hull
constant as recursive
— a room of one vine —
tendril, sentiment with a calculating self-regard, contrast entwined
waste and use
timeless in valence.
John Calhoun lived here with a cousin once removed;
Robert and Mildred Bliss were siblings.
A renaissance candle lights a mural of marble.

The museum of racial variety
white three god
the combination of persons and numbers make *intention*.
Combed tusks prevail into a stoning—white
as the difference in 'each' and 'every' natural mark.
He is reluctant to see the incompatible except as cavernous
humility which like the underworld has numbered drivers.
Tupaq Amaru named his inquisitor, accomplice.
Twins descend to one death and seven death, lawgivers.
They endure rattling house, razor house
ignore manikins mistaken for real death.
A deer-eared man blows a conch on a crouched doe.

A SHINING LOOM

From here we saw the wave from *behind*,
a fish ladder cut in the canal, many-plated coil of razors.
They swarm each stair trough,
jump
as sharp fins on bellies
spread — process, enjambment of sense and protection.

The canal is Washington. We step in the lock; in a plate window
salmon and trout
pincer. A man and woman separate.
A boat lowered in the lock.
Glass external circulation — from inside we watched them
beat, in one eye and out.

They are pulses, but the real current is continuous against it.
Channel and current
(the couple joins, and she smooths his wool coat — a Russian naval officer's —
carding
tenderness) a double gated water tent, separate
three-sheeted threads of still-reductable gears.

A speckled palm orders the wave in both directions
there
naked in a guise of humane clothes
centripetal collective practices loss, gold lined remains
motion thread.
Because politics for many is a watched room when one *is* the room

down a grass slope we spoke with anger and excitement
what helped Clinton and Bush be elected.
This
straight course may be turned back,
but is never circular.
It leaves a resin of event, rinsing separate claims.

CALUMNY/A LEAF POURED

Loose sacs fixed
phasmida to window
heterodoxy as availability.
A hinged mouth chewed a real stem; white
globes hung on green seams below
green more vivid than luminous.
Unless it copied a saw-marked edge
exposure

its thin legs a lens scratch
I guessed eggs. We stopped
the tape: a man learns his friend is dead,
alive, leavening aspiration in discord
war profiteer, rival, *Orson Welles*
murdering him in sewers below Vienna
a hive poured out of persuasion;
a hive of selves

imageless distinction the heart-leaf
and a long shaded stalk in a single self.
As in film autumn
is a cemetery, over the Raritan
canal, 'the canal dug by Irishmen' 1831–1834
who 'earned more than the unskilled laborer'
in cholera.
(The want spacing cannot share even blind care.)

Service is a flood between the one world
and exposed
insect frames.
Mexican immigrants in white Princeton;
a sod farm, green spools for developments
a cement plant remains
the canal invites
not enclosure but an unexpected direction of similarity,

leaves against the reflective tide — north.
Stemmed
recursiveness, a clear image but not voice,
loam covers unintentional dams
in bronchial fibers (beyond internal ken).
Close-fretted work
in cell-like mirroring
Washington crosses from thicker to thin stem

What Trenton Makes the World Takes;
labor is in what passes and remains.
As tendency of living forms
while its stem may not be reversed
on the window cramped hind legs peeled.
Impossibly it fell on a branch.
Cells of worldliness,
clear lids see animal need which is unseen.

THEY ARE SPED

An eagle by naked women with trident and eagle-helmet,
brutal in perspective as a calking, lucid rattle

'To the defenders of the Union, 1861–1865'
(a serial consciousness is downwind

the unconscious is serum in the wing).
Springing from the top — somehow a weed has found a way.

Rosettes tent up under the thick arch;
its capitals are eagles.

Frederick MacMonnies' plank-winged 'Victory' or 'Columbia'
is set forward

so creamy massiveness hesitates.
With sailors a black boy crouches at a mortar.

Monumental waveless sociability
Whitman's eagle in the library sees progress in attention

seven headed lithium
feather.

Reversing circular skaters
Witnesses, thick elastic sleeves and high white socks

peace in conflict
(not within war)

a man living with cancer or AIDS.
Wooden paddles, talented bagpipes, two dogs twist into four

sumac is ordinal.
Women in straw skirts

white painted faces
pose the question between *who are you supposed to be*

and *where are you from*;
blue green, vein-blue

where covenant with a middle invitation
marchers for Louima gathered.

Success and failure stamp out the sun each day
many suns in one day.

ERRAND OF SLATE

Elevated rails, loud copied *rightening*
is a train because there is no reason to be impelled—
one rail what is possible
one rail what happens—the slat of occurrence unlimited,
the milk of symmetry, and a blur across the rails
diastolic. Cypress Hills is next.
A woman is dozing; her hair is raked up, and her son is wide for the stroller.
The train turns a corner.
One car racks the angle of the next one
flowerpots on shaken windows
a car wash, white tar paper on pink
aluminum siding, as amelioration is not a voice
spadelike leaves in the fences,
some rehabilitated homes, meringue, a car horn
wires closing in tuning the rails.

The tracks seem almost like planks on a creek.
These houses are about grating—one white, top to cellar.
Doves plate them up.
'You have to put your hand down *here*,'
says a worker stringing a lamp.
'He had to let them catch it by coming after him.'
'Then you could be king (widening arm circles)!' 'It stands for my money.'
A man sprays his driveway.
At the national cemetery
Maimonides, Mt. Zion, Union Field
courage lies between lives, as in each. Soldiers in rows as radiating streets
a massive cypress and summer
regular lines, a hill over tracks
and marshes of Jamaica Bay; the eye is alive with no course.

PRIOR

We ate a 'nice' salad.
Purple-seeded calamari; goat vertebrae and hanging tail the same fur as the rabbit,
generality with intricacy. Arthur Avenue
moves surgical supplies — trusses — 'we now have hot dogs!'
grappa in leonine grassiness, meteoric chokes.
A carnival game — double bets each miss — promises
returns (with enough cash) asymmetry
a concord-given arrow sharing in series with gain.
The barker gives a stuffed dog in consolation.
'Little Italy in the Bronx: The Good Taste of Tradition' —
as memorable these terms, the sere will make hunger
shell or bone curved in dismissing virtue,
a yard with speedboat fenced in — like the zoo.

A red and white sailcloth
is exposition, alternating red and white vinegar vats.
Livers pool in the tray three deep, a springy smell of dough
fish heads also hacked, green scungilli,
communion, hearts the size of melons.
Contamination is not combination, but inhuman hazard — a surety
with low entrance: Kosova studio, 'La Gringa,' Hallal markets
even in ethnic succession, find residual focus.
'in loving memory of anton d. nikki,' a double-headed eagle — a bugs bunny
freed within time and willing in vain passivity.
Halved conch, blue honeycomb tripe, winged bacalo
a market hopes to condition uncertainty and in calculating
grain, what is grown separately.
Although its contradiction may be seen by definition
eye muscle in a stripped calf cannot make visible
convincing that sated
a skin within meat.

A window is busy for constancy.
We shared *where* wonder grew radical in end-wonder
McDonald's Italia, Weber's pig feet, $2.00/lb of snails
unimodal between bodily awareness and competence.
The denunciation is as limited as the yearning — 'I'm going to break this ball.'
St. Barnabas Hospital in high front
striates direction, sacrifice in regularity.
'Nice' is no disposition. Mussels starve the oyster on its shell.

SELF-TAUGHT

A bulbous tower is lit with Christmas strings
similarity against dissimilarity against sight
elephants with human bodies, not humans with elephant heads.
A Buick is fins up in a driveway, window
horse and carriage shutter-stenciled — conveyances,
the toy school bus wreck, lattice and vine shoots
from Old Country. Location is between invention
and incarceration. A man says 'ma' to his dog.
A house perpendicular 'stands,' identity
as segment self-concealing analogy. A cat is wrapped like a boxer.
Laburnum, Mulberry, trees with mineral lancing
amid uncertainty, share a certain reserve.

Korean churches, lawn Madonnas, Jesus with snowmen flock
secular immersion finds sacred glass.
Three Sivas, radial day forward and backward
Ganesha's wide lap is robed silver and gold.
A five headed wave, civilization is span-limiting;
having doubled back it continues. Two women pray.
As world insecurities make ten anticipation
preemptive, fissive — but local survival as continuity atomizes
long-eyed relief, the irritant of sustainability.
Immature blessings never survive the obscene;
Ganesha gives time to compose.

Variegated is not variety. A calligraphic tower past Kissena Park
contrasts self-delivered lines
in secrecy. Behind the Botanic Garden
a t'ai chi leader smiles at a white woman
moving not at the same rate but with the illusion of a page.

He is startled when she shouts
'ExerCISE. We all exerCISE.'
Juxtaposition is classicism; next to *and* with
(a wide-ribboned knot) is equality.

SOLSTICE

Kill van Kull stair pipes
music,
Williamsburg Savings, World Trade Center
a contact of sound and spar
vertical then humility-wavering toil
access is virtue and virtue is definition,
a summer explanation.
Between clear blue and spines of the Goethals
one heron glides over an empty sanctuary.
Horizontal
two billion gallons containers Jersey
clouds over green water, sun on less transparent blue
caustic wash, water wash, refineries
a winter hive
revisits an internal register when collective coherence
erases continuity in a simple weave.
The wake brushes yellow foam.
A crabbed flame, a yellow crane
where water and current seeded oysters
from New England to Chesapeake.

A white peahen with reed fan tufts
the Chinese Scholars' Garden
is the 'only authentic classical
Chinese Garden in the United States'
circumventing straight traveling ghosts
sea-star green.
A bronze scholar rides a rooster;
variety in uniformity
a clay army protects the dead.

A 'pavilion of insight for fish,'
'terrace of crispness — Bell Atlantic'
negative, space
gives authority forestalled commitment.
Hexagons on triangles shadow as symmetry
seclusion which can become only energy.

Ken Saro-Wiwa's lawyer wrote 'the sour
mangrove tide,' but memorial exists with development
a rack of song-starred gourds.
A rising winter issue,
the summer leaves its circulating gain.
The heron lands where no one planted.
Where the living share a common claim
music is not a second help for the dead.
I realized I was always the same as now
a strain.
Kuru the tortoise, the laugher, 'Kuru goes hungry again.'